Speak That We May Know

ALSO BY JUSTUS GEORGE LAWLER:

The Christian Imagination (Newman-Paulist)
The Catholic Dimension in Higher Education
    (Newman-Paulist)
The Range of Commitment (Bruce-Macmillan)
The Christian Image (Duquesne University Press)
Nuclear War (Newman-Paulist)
Celestial Pantomime (Yale University Press)
Odium Theologicum (forthcoming)

Religious Art in the Twentieth Century,
    by P. R. Régamey, translated with an Introduction
    (Herder and Herder)
The Challenge of Mater et Magistra, editor
    (Herder and Herder)
*Makers of the Catholic Community: Historical Studies
    on the Catholic Church in America, 1789–1989,*
    six volumes, literary editor (Macmillan)

Speak That We May Know

A SPIRITUALITY FOR UTTERING THE INNER YOU

Justus George Lawler

MEYER
STONE
BOOKS

Published in the United States by Meyer-Stone Books, a division of Meyer, Stone, and Company, Inc., 2014 South Yost Avenue, Bloomington, IN 47403

Cover design: Carol Evans-Smith

Typesetting output: TEXSource, Houston

Manufactured in the United States of America
92 91 90 89 88   5 4 3 2 1

Library of Congress Cataloging in Publication Data

Lawler, Justus George.
    Speak that we may know.

    1. Spirituality. I. Title.
BV4501.2.L359   1988   248   88-42726
ISBN 0-940989-41-7

For
Richard Roberts Lawler

Contents

Foreword

THIS VERY CONDENSED, YET EASY TO READ BOOK is a wonderful antidote to what Matthew Arnold calls "This strange disease of modern life / With its sick hurry, its divided aims." Nothing is easier than to experience life as "one damn thing after another," to live permanently under the pressure to meet induced needs and imposed standards. Nothing is easier than to forget ourselves. Simply to experience myself as being is to feel the being of all there is, the mystery that being is. And no one who has ever had this experience will ask what is the use of it.

But how do we have this experience? That is what this book is about. And it is not a how-to book. "How do I get it?" is in the same order of questioning as "What use is it?" The proper question is "How am I getting it, now, without realizing it?" Justus George Lawler points us to the many occasions in life when the experience can occur, the things in the structure of our existence that create space for it. He has a fine knack for pointing up these looseners of our compact triviality.

The primary one is language. On the potential surprises and revelation in language, Lawler is second to

no author I know. He has written a superb book on
this, *Celestial Pantomime,* the main insights of which
the present work makes available to an audience less
specialized so far as literature is concerned. There are
wonderful moments, as when he points out (a thing I
had never noticed) that in the famous description of
Cortez staring for the first time on the Pacific ("Silent
upon a peak in Darien") the real point is in the line
"While all his men looked at each other." For there is
nothing private about the moment of light. It is precisely the moment when the mystery that enlivens and
binds us all together is felt in each.

In a way, the whole paradox of human existence —
its infinity and its total contingency — lies in language,
which both opens on infinity when used by the poet
and mutes the connection in ordinary functional speech.
There is a well-known debate as to whether language is
"conventional" — that is, a tool for communicating —
or "natural," expressing our radical connectedness with
the world. Anyone who thinks that this question could
ever be settled, has not got the point about being in the
world: we both are, simply and timelessly, and are busy,
and this divided existence shows itself in the uses of our
language.

This book, however, does not simply pass in review
the various "places" where the infinite shows itself. It
develops. There is a steady unfolding of the central
theme, concluding with the revealing linguistic break of
Rimbaud that has always haunted me: *Je est un autre,*
I is another. There are always further depths to the
self: below "it" as touched in prayer this morning there
is more, and below that there is more, and so on ad

infinitum — the realization that carried Etty Hillesum through the nightmare of the Nazis ending in the gas-chambers.

Finally, this is a timely book. We are experiencing the breakup of a culture based on ignoring the timeless dimension of consciousness and regarding the person as an isolated monad associating by choice with other monads. Almost every day, now, I sense the impossibility of this notion, and look out (and in!) on the ravages it creates in our world. Lawler highlights the crucial and salvific difference between the world in true perspective and the world not in true perspective. What I find so fascinating is that the effect of accentuating this difference is to dissolve the dualism of mind and body as we have it from Descartes, the philosophic father of the dread state we are in. No denigration of the body is involved in what Lawler has to say about our materialistic way of living. Quite the contrary, the body has been restored to it its proper existence, which is to mediate spirit and make love.

I have hardly touched on the many fine things in this book, to which I welcome the reader.

SEBASTIAN MOORE

Preface

THIS IS A BOOK about what makes each of us to be what she or he uniquely is. It is about the tension we all suffer between what we *appear* to be and what we *really are*. It is about how to heal that tension, how to resolve that conflict between appearance and reality, between *doing* and *being*.

Since one of the most powerful manifestations of that tension and of its resolution is language, this is also a book about words and speech and pre-eminently about that speech which we all unknowingly use when, however briefly, we experience the complete integration of ourselves so that appearance *is* reality, and reality *is* appearance. That speech of "wholeness" is what we call poetry, though it may have nothing to do with rhyme, rhythm, imagery, etc.

Since "wholeness" is identical with "holiness," this is also a book about religion. It thus is a small synthesis of the three kinds of knowledge most necessary to self-understanding and self-development in the context of our relation to the world about us, to other persons, and to God. This combination of theology, psychology, and philology makes this a book of what is traditionally called "spirituality."

I have conceived of this book as a series of meditations or reflections. Both of these words bear examination. "Meditation" is rooted in the term "mete" or "measure," that is, a meditation is the considering of or thinking about something that is presented to us not in its possibly overwhelming totality, but presented to us one brief portion at a time. Hence what follows is intentionally a short subject under each of the separate titles.

These are not chapters; that would be to suggest something very formal and even "bookish," in the negative sense of that word. Furthermore, all speech is measured, that is, is itself broken up into separate and brief segments, which is why we refer to articulate (meaning separable) language. But poetic speech is measured language in its highest form. It relies on meter, on a certain "beat" or "pulse" that affects us not by reasoning, not by thought, but by some kind of trans-rational rhythm that our *whole* being responds to — and it is with *wholeness* that we are concerned throughout everything that follows.

The second term I have used above is "reflection." It means simply that we see something in both its direct form, and its indirect; we see it as it is in the apparently objective world, and we see it as it is in some kind of subjective world. The reflecting mirror is a traditional accompaniment of the poet and of poetry — as Tennyson's "Lady of Shalott" makes beautifully clear. Thus in the act of reflecting, we are again drawing things into a wholeness, whether we consider that wholeness as a combination of objective and subjective, of thing and image, of reality and reflection.

The book assumes that the human person is on a journey, that her very existence is a journey that has a beginning and that is seeking an end, a destination and a destiny. Since existence is a quest, the book begins with a simple question, and ends with a simple answer to that question. And since that answer, as every answer, is implicit in the question, it becomes clear that the journey we are engaged in is circular: we have gone away from our home with a view to returning to it. And when we reach "home" we know it is a place of wholeness and holiness.

In these introductory observations, I want to introduce a classic and familiar poem that will illustrate what I have just said. This poem will also serve to exemplify the "method" in the reflections that follow. Wordsworth has a "journey" poem — we will examine it in more detail later — about a vision of the city of London that surprises him by its beauty.

> Earth *has* not anything to show more fair,
> Dull would he be of soul who could pass by
> A sight so touching in its majesty.
> This city now *doth* like a garment wear
> The beauty of the morn....

As I shall discuss later the journey theme is brought out by the three lines that keep us in a state of suspense as to precisely what the poet has seen. This is the suspense we all feel when on a long trip or voyage we are simply "passing the time of day" until we arrive at our destination. We are engaged quite literally in "pedestrian" activity, somewhat aimlessly, somewhat pointlessly in a state of suspension until we reach our goal. Then suddenly, unexpectedly the sight of that goal surprises us, just as at the end of the three long lines of wandering, we are surprised by the outburst, "*This* city." The journey itself may be banal, and ordinary, and to describe it we use banal and ordinary language. "Earth *has* not anything...." It is this and the other verb I have italicized that are revelatory.

One would expect the poet just for reasons of euphony, of sonic harmony, to say, "ear*th* ha*th*" — but he doesn't. He uses ordinary language for the ordinary event. But when he comes to his surprising vision, which is for him the entire goal of his pedestrian effort, which is for him the long-anticipated sacred moment, he unconsciously employs what we all recognize as liturgical language: "city *doth*." Nothing else can explain this shift in the use of these verbs. They move from profane to sacred.

That is what we shall be doing in the pages that follow. We feel instinctively that the poet — unlike, say, the businessman, the lawyer, etc. — does not manipulate language to her own ends. We instinctively think of the poet as being "inspired," as moved to speak by something that is "above" or "over" her. The poet is not a scientist or philosopher who is consciously working through some kind of puzzle and then setting forth in precise terms the answer. Rather, the poet, we feel, intuitively responds to the depths of reality, to the mystery at the core of people and nature, and in that response reflects that mystery. "Has" and "does" are the language of the marketplace, of pedestrian activity: "hath" and "doth" are the language of the holy and the whole.

This is the quest of this book. To travel through the ordinary, through the pedestrian and banal, in order to reach the sacred, to reach what traditionally has been called "the heavenly Jerusalem": "This city now *doth* like a garment wear the beauty...."

One word more. In order to avoid any kind of sexist language, I have randomly used masculine and feminine grammatical forms as well as examples and illustrations. To avoid the clumsy construction that such non-sexist language often entails, I have generally used the first person, singular or plural, to refer to women and men collectively, and have referred to the deity as "Thou" or "It" and thus as beyond gender differentiation.

Acknowledgments

No PART OF THIS BOOK has appeared in print else-where, but it is based on several published studies and is indebted to a number of authors and friends. Among the former, and the pertinent fields of focus, are:

For theology: *The Journal of the American Academy of Religion; Worship; The Anglican Theological Review; Continuum; The Journal of Religion; Jubilee; New Blackfriars; Commonweal; Christian Century.*

For psychology: *The Review of Metaphysics; Clio, An Interdisciplinary Journal; Psychiatry; Journal for the Study of Interpersonal Processes; The Month; Journal of Arts and Letters.*

For literary theory and criticism: *Modern Language Quarterly; Encounter* (U.K.); *Thought; College English; Continuum.*

My debt to the following is long-standing, and personal, academic, and professional: Thomas Altizer for consistency; Marianne Bankert for *Continuum* and the long time; Ellen Arl and Susan Breen for *hilaritas;* Anne Carr for balance; Paula Cooey for new support; Robert Daley for resolution; Chris Downing for depth; Langdon Gilkey for guts; Dick Horsley for social light; Ray

Hart for loyalty; Chris Kauffman and family for counsel and refuge; Julia Lawler for holding things together; Werner Linz and the team for homecoming; Matt Lamb and Sebastian Moore for "doing" *Celestial Pantomime* and so suggesting this little book; Tom and Pat McMahon for being here; Margaret Miles for editorial confidence; Mary Lou O'Grady for enjoying typing the ms. through the good offices of Maureen Scott, Dean preeminent; Jane Schaberg for courage and intellect; Elisabeth and Francis Schüssler Fiorenza for over two decades in the cause; Marjorie Suchocki for good timing; David Tracy for Order; Paul van Buren for character. To all the above for all of this.

This little work is dedicated to my third son, Rich; his two brothers, Tom and George, have had their books earlier. The marvel of the three, a poet, an artist, a musician, makes me never cease to wonder at the miracle of it all. Lastly, like everything I have ever written, I owe this to Josephine Schriber Lawler.

JUSTUS GEORGE LAWLER
April 12, 1988

1

Waiting Is Being

FEW THINGS ARE MORE TRITE than those old catechism answers that many of us remember, answers that were exhaustively analyzed and dissected by teachers and preachers when we were children. And these are answers that are still lodged in our memory where they may on the one hand startle us by their insight or, on the other hand and more frequently, may merely sound like dull and meaningless echoes from the past.

To the question, "Why did God make us?" the answer comes trotting off the tongue usually without the least reflection: "to know, love, and serve God in this world, and to be happy with God in the next world." We have heard these words so often they no longer provoke thought. Nevertheless, at some time after we had memorized this answer so that as children we knew it by rote, it is likely that the oddity of the answer must have struck us. Because it is in fact a most curious statement. We extinguishable, frangible, in many ways negligible,

21

creatures do something *for God,* so that in some strange sense God has need for us, or at least wants us to feel that there is a need for us on God's part.

What we do is know and love God. This all seems fairly conventional, even though it seems so only because the words "know and love" have become stereotypes. Nevertheless knowing and loving seem like spontaneous, even automatic processes, processes that happen naturally as a flower will follow the sun through the sky. But "serving" brings in an entirely different category of activity, and it is only because we have so often heard the three terms, "know, love, serve," joined together in this catechism formula that we lose sight of the oddity of this third word. Knowing and loving are the basis for everything personal from human life to the life of the Trinity. But "serving"...?

"They also serve who only stand and wait," is a statement by Milton that, like the catechism's answer, has almost lost its power to shock or surprise; it too has almost become a stereotype. But Milton is suggesting a rarely noticed distinction between the angels, who according to the Bible serve God by *doing* God's bidding, and people, here represented by the blind poet, who serve God not by doing but merely by *being.* This is what the Jewish mystic, Simone Weil—who nurtured her spirituality on the writings of one of Milton's contemporaries, George Herbert—called *"attente de Dieu,"* literally a "waiting upon God" (Pascal). We serve God not by doing, but simply by being, by being what we are in the deepest way possible.

There are three cardinal terms in that last statement: "being," "are," and "deepest," and each of these terms is closely related. When we say we serve God by simply *being,* this does not imply some kind of inertness or passivity. It means we now exist in a state of heightened "isness"; what makes us to be what uniquely we alone *are* is now intensified.

In a certain sense we can say in these moments of *attente de Dieu* that "only now am I truly I." Only now is my unique I-ness being exercised, being activated, being enlivened and made manifest. And we recognize that this I-ness, which makes me to be what I alone am, resides in my "deepest" center. In the very act of "serving" God we come to experience our self. In fact, the only way we can encounter the core of our own deepest, purest reality is when we are simply being in the presence of Being. (All language is metaphoric, all language fails; poets and mystics are mumblers. This use of "being/Being" has been criticized on — extraneous — philosophical grounds, and we shall look at some of those criticisms shortly. It is enough to say for now that the terms are serviceable both conceptually and empirically. "Being is used of any transcendent ultimate and, by indirection, of God.)

The most intense experience of our own being occurs in the relationship with transcendent Being, that is, in the relationship with truth, goodness, beauty, and personhood. In the moment of encounter with any one or all of these participations of Being, we know immediately and directly what we ourselves really are.

When we are involved in the everyday, ordinary distracting activities of living, when we are riding the bus, going shopping, etc., in response to the question, "What are you doing?" we could say *exactly* what we are *do-ing*. But in an encounter with a truly good person whose very presence moves us, in an encounter with the beautiful, say, a splendid sunset viewed in the presence of a good friend — in these encounters if someone asked us, "What are you doing?" the answer would be quite different. In these moments of meeting the true, the good, the beautiful, we are really not doing anything. We simply *are*. And we have an experience of our is-ness in an intensified way as it is excited, animated, correlated to Is-ness outside of us. We experience our own being; we experience what makes us to be our-selves. In these moments a person can say, "Now I am *I*." "This is the real I in a way that I was not really my deepest, truest self when caught up in the trivia of everyday living, when riding the bus, going shopping, etc."

In these moments when we truly *are* ourselves, we have a twofold experience. We experience Being draw-ing us out of the prison of aloneness — so to speak — an experience which depending on its content and its in-tensity we may call "ecstasy" or "education." And sec-ondly in the very act of being drawn out, we experience the beauty and richness of our own being, the beauty and richness of our own unique selfness.

Now, these are *experienced* realities; they cannot be taught to us, they cannot be taken on the testimony of someone else; they can only be experienced person-ally and interiorly. We recognize this experience by what happens within ourselves. We "discern our true spirit" — to use an old phrase from religious writers. We discover "our better selves" — to use an old phrase from folk wisdom. We feel a sense of *self*-security, not in the sense of safeness, smugness, introspectiveness, but in the sense that our *selfness,* what makes us to be truly and uniquely what we are, is experienced.

In this moment there is no longer a discrepancy between what we are and what we do. There are no discrepancies, no divisions, no dualities; there is no sense that *this* is a bodily experience or that *this* is a mental experience. It is an experience of the "I" joined to all other "I's" and somehow joined as well to some *ultimate* "I." In Keats's poem on Chapman's Homer, Cortez the explorer is described as staring at the Pacific, "while all his men looked *at each other.*" In the moment of encountering the transcendent, each isolated being (*esse*) becomes joined in community, becomes a "co-being" (*coesse*).

In these moments of the "I" experience, in these moments when one can say now I really *am* myself — and we must remember that "am," "are," "is," are all being (*esse*) verbs — there is no longer a barrier between myself and this other person, or between myself and the "world." This is akin to what theologically was called the gift of integrity: I am an integer, a whole number, no longer a fraction — a fraction being something that has been fractured, broken, bent, pulled in two different directions. I am now one with myself, with the other person, with nature, and ultimately with supreme Being.

All then becomes *one,* being flows in and through me. This is what the mystics call a state of porosity; it is more than mere openness to being, since openness implies some kind of opening, some kind of passage from outside to inside or inside to outside. But here there is

no "out" or "in" — all is one great breathing, one great
pulse moving through all reality, which while conjoining us to that reality also makes us more uniquely our
individual selves.

2

The Return to the Garden

THIS POROSITY, THIS EXPERIENCE of one great breath of being flowing through ourselves and through all reality, is what is meant by the story of Adam and Eve in Eden. That story tells us of the condition we are destined for, a condition that we can now experience only fitfully and occasionally. Adam and Eve, each of these two ideal types or models, is one with himself or herself, one with each other, one with nature and animal creation, and one with God.

But after the "fall," barriers are erected, everything becomes separated off from everything else. This is what is symbolized by the fig leaf; this is what is symbolized by the end of nakedness. They now *appear* different on the "outside" from what they *are* on the "inside." Appearance and reality are in conflict, and they become living lies — a lie being defined precisely as this conflict. They now put on a façade, a "front," which not only conceals their "within," but which acts as a shield, as an aggressive obstacle to everything outside of them. In this state, every "other" is truly the enemy.

This is a state if *dis*-integration. There is a discrepancy between appearance and reality, between their "doing," relating them to the external world, and their "being," relating them to their interiority. The first consequence of this "fall" is that they quarrel with one another; similarly the animals and the soil rebel against them; and finally they are estranged from Being itself. Thus is lost the primordial unity and integrity of all reality. But it is precisely this sense of such a loss that drives them, compels them, to seek to restore that original state.

In those moments when we strip away the façade, the "front," the clothing, in those moments when we *do* nothing, but simply let things *be,* in those moments we experience once again the ancient longed-for oneness with ourselves, with each other, with nature, and with God.

"Clover is ethereal fingerpointing," said Keats, by which he meant that the sight of a beautiful field is a guidepost on the way to union with the ultimate. When we encounter beauty — or rather when it encounters us — so long as we place no obstacle to this epiphany of being, so long as we can let the mask and façade, the "clothing" drop away, then in that moment once again our being is drawn out of us, being enters us, and we resonate to one universal chord of Being. We experience again the melding, the blending together — the experience the mystics call a *conjunctio,* a conjoining.

For the adult, as Keats intimated, it is frequently the phenomenon of beauty that initiates this ecstatic experience of being, and it is this experience that tells us that there is meaning, significance to our own being and to the being of the universe. The seeming emptiness, pointlessness, nothingness of existence is contradicted by the ecstatic experience of the beautiful. "Earth's ignorant nullity made strange by flowers," says the poet Siegfried Sassoon. For children, unlike adults, who cannot articulate their experience (in-fant = non-speaking), it is more likely the experience of the good as mediated by the love of their parents and the beneficence of their protected environment that engenders this experience of wholeness.

But in fact there should be no sharp distinction made between these various manifestations of being since the difference between beauty, truth, and goodness is somewhat artificial. Thomas Aquinas spoke of beauty as the "splendor of truth," and Walter Benjamin spoke of moral goodness as well as of the beautiful work of art as having an "aura," a common splendor or radiance. But it is probably that each transcendental expression of being affects us differently at different ages and under different circumstances.

3

The Two Great Sadnesses

WE HAVE SEEN THAT IT IS THIS SENSE of discrepancy between what we do and what we are, between appearance and reality, that is the motive force that impels us to seek unity. This is what the ancients called *eros,* and what St. Paul from a different perspective called the love of Christ that drives us and urges us (*urget nos*) forward. This is a sadness that we feel as a strain, as a tension drawing us in two directions, and that might be called the latent schizophrenia we are all of us heir to. But it is a sadness that, like physical pain, gives us as well an insight into our condition, a warning of our schizoid nature, while also providing a motive for seeking a "cure." Poets have described this erotic urging (and "erotic" here does not mean radically sexual, though there may be an initial sexual component) in the figure of *"la belle dame sans merci,"* the lovely lady who is thankless or pitiless. In this sense she is a manifestation of Being itself, described in a now-classic definition as the fascinating and the terrifying. We shrink in pain from this terrible tension within ourselves, yet this tension is a blessing inasmuch as it compels us to seek resolution in wholeness and oneness.

The other sadness, paradoxically, comes upon us precisely when we have experienced such wholeness. It is more mysterious, or at least more psychologically confusing, because it is almost a concomitant or accompaniment of ecstasy. That the strain of contending dualities (appearance-reality, doing-being, etc.) should cause sadness is hardly surprising; that ecstatic wholeness should bring with it its own kind of sadness can be upsetting, even dumbfounding.

The ancients, writing out of a totally patriarchal tradition, stated that every animal except woman experiences sadness after sexual union. The rampant masculine bias here need not detain us, but there is a truth in the observation that has nothing to do with conventional notions that every "high" entails a "let down," or that every moment of bliss involves sadness simply because the moment must pass. The sadness we are considering here is much more profound than this, and goes far beyond the sexual, so that it is true to say that such sadness or melancholy is a concomitant of every ecstatic experience whether it be the encounter with beauty, with truth, or with goodness.

The explanation is that in each such ecstatic experience our very is-ness is, as it were, intensified, reanimated. Unlike the world of doing, making, and having, unlike the world of business where we really are not our true self, in these experiences of being, these experiences of being what we uniquely *are,* we have a kind of immediate intuition of our very is-ness, an intuition, we might say, of the very nature of our "soul," or "spirit," or "selfness" — all these words are metaphors for the undefinable. In this intuition we recognize that "soul," that "being," for what it radically is, something utterly contingent, something that does not have an absolute hold on Being, something that could be, as it were, snuffed out in a moment. And this intuitive and immediate sense of the essential fragility of what we *are* fills us with the deepest existential sadness. ("Sadness" is the right word; "anguish" suggests something too sharp, too penetratingly painful.) What we experience is a kind of all-pervading emptiness, a kind of vastation, as the mystics would call it, coming from the recognition of our sheer contingency. Says Keats, "in the very temple of *delight,* veiled *melancholy* has her sovereign shrine." This is the melancholy we experience in the ecstatic encounter of being with Being.

Within the mystical tradition this "melancholy" is akin to what John of the Cross describes as the dark night of the senses, a darkness that falls upon us after the first great illumination of being. It is a theme that comes most articulately into our literature with the first Romantic poets. Keats's "Ode to a Nightingale" begins with four lines that are the very embodiment of this "sadness" of contingency:

> My heart aches, and a drowsy numbness pains
> My sense, as though of hemlock I had drunk,
> Or emptied some dull opiate to the drains
> One minute past, and Lethe-wards had sunk....

The next statement is totally unexpected. The cause of

this interior devastation is the poet's ecstatic *delight* in the symbolic song of the bird: *"being too happy in thy happiness."* This says everything: it is the intensity of the happiness that generates the heartaches and numbness.

Wordsworth spells it out more prosaically, but perhaps thereby all the more effectively in "Resolution and Independence":

> But, as it sometimes chanceth, from the might
> Of joy in minds that can no further go,
> As high as we have mounted in delight
> In our dejection do we sink as low;...

Delight/dejection; first the delight, then concomitantly the dejection. Lastly, Coleridge in the conclusion to "Christabel" describes one of the results of this sense of delight/dejection — a bitterness that taints everything we do and say:

> And pleasures flow in so thick and fast
> Upon his heart, that he at last
> Must needs express his love's excess
> With Words of unmeant bitterness

Perhaps the paradox of "the second great sadness" can be comprehended by taking the opposite approach. One of our perennial puzzles is about the attractiveness of tragedy, or about the appeal of certain works of art that we think of as being basically "ugly"; examples are innumerable in our time, the cacophonies of Stravinsky, Picasso paintings, Giacometti sculptures, etc. The question is why this attractiveness, why this undeniable appeal? One explanation — which I proffer only to clarify the larger issues broached above of existential sadness — is that the encounter with these works of art so excites our being, so intensifies our sense of is-ness, that what we experience is less the art work as such than our own selfness, our own "soul." And it is the beauty of that "soul," glimpsed immediately and intuitively, that accounts for the feeling of esthetic pleasure elicited even by works of art that are objectively "ugly."

That "soul" will also be concomitantly recognized as rooted in *contingency,* as in the analysis above, and will therefore also generate the existential sadness described above.

But this second sadness, like the first, acts as a motive force for us to reach out to being more ardently, to seek the ever deeper experience of our contingent is-ness relating to absolute Is-ness.

4

More in God than in Ourselves

I REPEAT THE FUNDAMENTAL AXIOM. In these encounters with the transcendent, we cannot say what we are doing; we are not *doing* anything, we are simply *being*. In ordinary, everyday activities, as we have noted, one can say, yes, I am doing this or that: I am working, I am jogging, etc. But in these ecstatic-educative experiences, all one can say is, now I truly am, I am being *I*, I am I in a deeper sense than when working, jogging, etc. I am truly now my real self, as I was *not* truly my real self when caught up in the world of business and activity.

Here we recognize the strange paradox of being's relation to Being. To the degree that I am absorbed in the being around me, absorbed in this beautiful, true, good, or deeply personal reality, my own sense of truly being *I* is intensified and deepened. To the degree that I am totally given over to being "outside" of me, drawn into it, enticed by it, to that degree the being "inside" of me is more fully *its true self.* To the degree I pour myself out, to that degree do I become more fully myself. To the degree I lose myself in the "other," to that degree I find my authentic self.

That is the meaning of the mystical maxim, "we exist more fully in God than we exist in ourselves." But the implication of this is startlingly paradoxical: to the degree that my existence is *more fully in God* to that degree is my own existence *more fully in me.* Erich Fromm in *The Art of Loving* has emphasized that this principle is true not only of mystical love, but of human sexual love as well — in fact, the distinctions between mystical and sexual love are mainly a matter of degree rather than a matter of kind. Fromm noted a universal phenomenon of the relation of self and other: the more the lovers expend themselves for the beloved, the more the lovers pour themselves out for the beloved, the more the lovers then become their true selves. This is the meaning of the Gospel saying: unless the grain of wheat fall into the ground and die, itself remaineth alone. But if it willingly dies into the other, then the more fully it lives and is no longer alone.

Thus as one loses one's individuality in the transcendent, one becomes more profoundly individualized. This is an essential notion in all Western religion and contrasts with much Eastern thought, in which the finite is simply absorbed by the infinite. Thus the oriental mystic and poet Shankara declares: "My mind dropped like a hailstone into God's infinite ocean and melted and joined with him." This can be contrasted with another poet and mystic, Gerard Manley Hopkins, who suggested:

> Suppose God showed us in a vision the whole world inclosed first in a drop of water, allowing everything to be seen in its native colors; then the same in a drop of Christ's blood, by which everything whatever was turned scarlet, *keeping nevertheless* mounted in the scarlet *its own color too.*

One can go even further and intensify the paradox by affirming that not only is the self not extinguished in the absolute ("keeping its own color too") but, when joined to the absolute, the self becomes more truly itself, that is, its own "color" becomes richer, fuller, etc. Similarly the poet Wallace Stevens, who embraced Christianity on his deathbed, inquires at the end of "The Idea of Order at Key West," as to why "the glassy lights, / The lights in the fishing boats... / Mastered the night... Arranging, *deepening,* enchanting night." As the light arranges the night, it also *deepens* it: the light makes the dark "more" dark.

Such a deepening of one's individuality when it is absorbed by the "other" is also brought out in the Western tradition by the emphasis on one's proper name in relating to the nameless One, God. Thus, according to the Jewish mystical authors of the Kabbalah, each of the people who fled from Egypt with Moses continues to subsist individually in the universal community of Israel, and each has a uniquely personal relationship with the Godhead: "To none other than he, whose soul springs from thence, will it be given to understand God in this special and individual way that is reserved to him." And according to Isaac Luria, one of the masters of the Kabbalah, in the Messianic age "every single man in Israel will read the Torah [i.e., encounter the Godhead] in accordance with the meaning peculiar to his root." And like Hopkins's "self," which retains its unique "color" when engulfed by the universal "color" of Being, Isaac Luria adds, "And thus also is the Torah understood *in Paradise.*" Even in "heaven" the individual will not be lost in the Absolute.

In Western theology individuality and selfness must not be lost because the expression of that individuality and selfness is the very reason for the creature's existence. We are back to the catechism question, "Why did God make me?"

Human being is finite and limited; Supreme Being is infinite. If that Supreme Being is to share Herself with others, that is, if that Supreme Being is to communicate Himself infinitely, it must find expression in a near infinitude of lesser beings. Thus it is the destiny of each human person to manifest some unique aspect of the infinite nature of Supreme Being. Every human person, then, is created in order to express his or her utterly original, utterly different, utterly unique nature. The world of human beings is an almost infinitely multicolored spectrum, no shade or tint of which is the same as any other shade or tint. But all of them fused together throughout the expanse of time manifest the pure luminescent radiance of Supreme Being. The human vocation, then, is not endless imitation, is not endless conformity, endless sameness. The human vocation is to be true to the unique is-ness breathed into us at birth; it is to be what we truly *are,* and to intensify and deepen that is-ness by relating it to absolute Is-ness.

5

Apocalypse

GRAMMAR IS GLAMOUR is an old saying that suggests that language has a kind of bewitching charm that moves us when we are least aware of it. Words are very much like persons; they have an outside, a surface meaning, and also a hidden dimension of depth that is only gradually discovered. As we move forward in our understanding of what can only be called a Christotherapoetics, I will rely more and more on certain aspects of language and of grammatical systems to clarify our progress.

The bedrock principle remains: we are able to fulfill ourselves, to be satisfied with ourselves, only to the degree that we are faithful to our unique is-ness, in sum that we *be* what we are. This is of course a very difficult attainment; it is that true philosophy — the experience of being — which Kant called "a herculean labor." We have noted that there are obviously times when we are less true to our real selves, times when we are engaged in a multiplicity of activities, when we are "*busy* about many things," as Jesus said of Mary of Bethany; there are times when we lose sight of the "one necessary" thing, that is, simply *being* what we are.

But there are also times when it *is* desirable to wear something of a "mask," to maintain a kind of façade, to keep the "fig leaf" in place. In a world where we are all vulnerable, the mask prevents ourselves from being wounded needlessly. Ideally, if we were saints, we should maintain our total openness. This is, as we shall see, in some ways the meaning of Jesus' life: the person who was so totally open that even to preserve his life against his enemies he would not dissimulate, would not wear the mask. This is the highest form of witness to being utterly what we are, but it is probably a form that is beyond the strength of many of us.

For most of us there are times when it is preferable not to expose casually to every newcomer, as it were, the nature of our interior reality. Most of us have felt a sense of mild revulsion or even of distinct repugnance at people who are always gushing forth their innermost thoughts and feelings, people who have so little sense of the sacredness of what they are that they divulge it on every inappropriate occasion. These are the people who, according to the old saying, "wear their hearts on their sleeve." Compulsively, almost by an uncontrollable act of the will they expose without any restraint or reverence everything about their inner reality. But in fact, what they expose is not their authentic selves — which can never be revealed by an act of will — but only some imaginary construction of what they envision their authentic selves to be.

The word "revelation" tells us that there is an "inner" reality and an "outer" reality that obscures — again, all spatial imagery is distorting, but it does convey a poetic sense of the situation. The "outer" reality is the "veil" that must be dropped if the inner reality is to be made manifest, if the inner reality is to shine through and transfigure the outer reality so that the human person is truly unified and integrated. Revelation is un-veiling; it comes about not by forcing, through an act of the will, the inner reality to be exposed; it comes about simply by the spontaneous response of our being to the richness of Being outside of us. That Being, whose transcendent expressions are truth, goodness, beauty, and personhood, that Being, as it were, calls to us. Being's word goes out from Itself and addresses our being, and we instinctively open ourselves (or rather, we are opened) to a response, to a re-ply. A re-ply is simply a bending back of ourselves to the Other.

This un-veiling is a free, unpredictable occurrence. As Stevens says, "it occurs as it occurs": it simply happens. The word of Being speaks to us, to our deepest self, speaks to what there is of us that is uniquely ourselves; it speaks to what we *are*. Being speaks to being, and being responds to Being. In this moment we know and love Being. This is revelation, this is apocalypse. The mythological maiden Calypso had long tresses that covered her face and body. When in the moment of love she brushed them aside, there occurred an unveiling, and what was unveiled was her true beauty in an apo-Calypso. However, it is not even accurate to say she "brushed" them aside. That suggests an act of the will. Rather one should say that her tresses parted in response to the gesture of love from the outside, and she stood revealed.

So, too, at the death of the utterly open person, Jesus: the veil of the temple was simultaneously rent signifying that the encounter with Being is something immediate and spontaneous, something that requires no elaborate preparations. The naked body of Jesus on the Cross is opened by the spear, and Being flows forth; the veil of the temple is rent, and we have access to Being.

Lastly, it is important to emphasize again that when we are speaking of being, we are not discussing some abstraction, some philosophical concept — though it may in some sense be these as well. It is necessary throughout this analysis to return incessantly to a consideration of our own is-ness. It is necessary to reflect on those experiences when we can ecstatically say, now I *am;* this *is* the true *I;* now I experience the very is-ness that makes me to be uniquely what I am.

6

Between Is-ness and Is-not-ness

Now, THE HUMAN BEING ALSO DWELLS in the world of "things," in the world of realities that in the radical sense are not truly is-nesses. Rather they have, as it were, a greater proportion of is-not-ness in their make up. We all recognize this, but rarely reflect upon it.

The difference between a tiny, ineffectual, and helpless infant and an efficient, splendidly appointed automobile is that the former has no price because it is of limitless worth, because it is in some sense infinite. This infinitude is what we experience when our being is drawn out of us. We go beyond the limbs that limit us and are in touch with all reality; the totality of existence breathes through us and we breathe through it. This unlimitedly valuable infant *is* in a way that the car is *not*. Thus the car that functions, aids us, is a kind of extension of us, is recognized to be more an is-not-ness than an is-ness.

Somewhere between the thing and the person, between the car and the infant is another mysterious world that shares in is-ness more than do mere things, but does not have that full richness of is-ness that defines the person. This is the world of animal reality. In Eden Garden before the fall, as paintings like "The Peaceable Kingdom" remind us, animals were not exploited by persons; rather the animals found their own slight hold on is-ness strengthened by relating to the far deeper is-ness of human beings.

Thus the animal is a twofold symbol reminding human beings, first, of Eden Garden and of that integrity and purity that they lost there. Even more, the animal is a symbol of humanity's undefiled image; for Adam and Eve's act of naming the animals was not an assertion of dominion over them. This naming represented human beings' companionship with that aspect of creation that had been created in their image even as human beings were created in the image of God. Hence the friendship of the great saints with the animals. The great saints preached to them, and the animals in the act of comprehending such "sermons" comprehended themselves and realized through the saints — the persons most akin to Eve and Adam before the fall — their place in a divine order of existence.

But if the animal is a symbol of what creation was in its state of innocence, it is also a symbol of what humanity is now in its state of estrangement. The piteous glance of the animal, of which Martin Buber has written so eloquently, comes from the fact that the animal cannot quite respond to being outside of itself. The animal's eyes express the frustration of an is-ness too diminished, too powerless to penetrate fully its material envelope. The emergence of is-ness in the animal is a momentary event, without transforming power and without endurability. But in this very frustration the animal speaks silently of the groaning and travailing of the whole of an expectant creation. So it was no exaggeration for Matthew Arnold to write of his dog:

> That liquid, melancholy eye,
> From whose pathetic, soul-fed springs
> Seemed surging the Virgilian cry,
> The sense of tears in mortal things.

Nor is it surprising that when Jesus went into the desert to fast and pray, the Gospel reports that he lived among animals and was ministered to by angels. Here we have a marvelous picture of the whole scale of is-ness. Jesus *as man* representing the fullest of *human* be-ing, of human is-ness; above him as man, the angels representing the fullest of transcendent created be-ing; finally, Jesus as man with the angels responding to the ultimate *Is*-ness in the universe. And at the foot of this whole staircase of is-ness rests the creature whose slight hold on is-ness struggles ceaselessly with the opacity of is-not-ness. Hence, lastly, the presence in so many religious paintings of animals, and the presence of animals at the birth of the infant Jesus.

7

Notness

T HE REALITY IN WHICH THERE IS NOT the least suggestion of is-not-ness, and the reality which is all Is-ness,
we call God. But there is only one way we can come
to know this ultimate Be-ing, and that way is the way
of experience. We must begin, again, by reflecting on
those experiences when we *are* truly ourselves, when we
experience a going beyond our ordinary limitations.

As we have seen, those experiences occur when we
are moved by the beauty of some natural phenomenon,
by the goodness of some other person, when we are
drawn out of ourselves and then know, immediately and
without consciously adverting to it, that now: I truly
am *I*. This is the *real* I. We then know interiorly and
intuitively what it is to be fully existing as our real self.
We also know that it is some Reality beyond ourself
that drew us out, that aroused, as it were, our latent is-
ness, woke it up "inside" us, so that we could feel that
is-ness in all its fullness. In that experience of what
we truly *are,* we experience the ultimate Is-ness that

aroused, awakened, excited us. We know God's Is-ness. We know God not as the conclusion to a syllogism and not as a hoped-for solution to our problems. We know God as the Is-ness that relates to our is-ness.

But we also know indirectly that there must be the possibility of some ultimate is-not-ness, or better, since it is a question of non-being, the possibility of some ultimate *notness*. This is the mystery of iniquity of which St. Paul writes. This too is an experienced knowledge. I do not mean experiential in the sense that we are always witness to some great evil in the world, or that we know historically of great evils perpetrated in the past. I mean that we experience in ourselves the lure of the destructive, the annihilative. This does not take the shape of some formally evil act or tendency, the kind of thing that would be against the law if discovered. This is evil in its more blatant manifestations, and as a rule is outside the experience of most people.

The lure of the destructive to which I refer more commonly takes the form of a lack of reverence for is-ness and the intentional frustration of the eros that drives others to pursue is-ness. It is the urge to dominate the very being of another person, usually a child, usually a spouse. It is the refusal to let this other person respond in his or her own way to his or her own unique mode of self-fulfillment. The very essence of being is freedom — a theme that runs through all of Nicholas Berdyaev's works — the very nature of is-ness is that it cannot be constrained, cannot be controlled, cannot be predicted or manipulated.

The only thing that can frustrate is-ness is is-not-ness. When we try to suppress another's is-ness, when we try to force it into our mold, we can do so only in the name of is-not-ness. This is the evil we experience in ourselves: the refusal to let another person *be* what she or he radically is.

There are other issues raised by the mystery of iniquity: if there is a personal principle of absolute is-ness called God, is there a personal principle of absolute notness? If there is a principle of absolute not-ness, must not its very negative "existence" finally be drawn into the order of positive existence when God is no longer so tolerant? And does this not imply that in the end, even evil, even a personal Satan, will be gathered into the final fulfillment of Is-ness. Such was the teaching of some Church Fathers, notably Origen, and such seems to be the teaching of John Paul II in a retreat preached before Pope Paul VI. But these are questions that fall outside the scope of this book.

The evil that we do experience is the desire to treat the sacred "other" as an object, not as a subject; as a thing that can be manipulated, not as a reality whose very essence is freedom. This evil reduces the person from something that pre-eminently *is* to something that pre-eminently *does*. It finds the significance of the person not in its intrinsic nature, but only in its extrinsic function. From that evil point of view the *role* one plays in society becomes more important than *what one is* in oneself. This functionalizing of persons, this manipulating of relations is the extinction of is-ness and the glorification of notness.

8

Being Is Oneness

W<small>E DWELL IN THE WORLD OF THINGS</small>, in the world
of realities that in the radical sense are not is-nessess,
and that therefore stand in opposition (or better stand
in counter-position) to human is-nesses in their struggle
to become what they truly are. The universe of things
is the universe of the fragmented and broken. It is a
universe where we are not truly "at home." Says Yeats,
"The wrong of unshapely things is a wrong too great to
be told."

We are seeking for oneness, and that oneness can
come only when we are being what we *are*. St. Thomas
says that "being and oneness are convertible," that is,
they imply each other. In those transcendent experiences when beauty, or truth, or goodness draws out our
very is-ness, then in those experiences we discover that
we are unified within ourself, with nature outside ourself, and with the supreme Is-ness. When we truly *are*,
then we are truly *one*. The tension between appear-

ance and reality, outside and inside, body and soul is resolved; there is no longer either the this *or* the that, there is only experienced oneness. "Soul and body have no bounds to lovers as they lie upon her tolerant enchanted slope," says W. H. Auden.

We live in a world of multiplicity and separability — what might loosely be called a world of "matter" — while being driven by a longing, an instinctive lure for the world of oneness and communion: what might loosely be called the world of "spirit." But we realize within ourselves that it is not a question of one element of the duality dominating the other: it is a question of the two merging, blending, melding.

We have already discussed the nature of this drive for the unlimited. It is the eros within, "the lovely figure who is pitiless," who is at once fascinating and awesome: it is Being itself that draws us to break through the barriers that confine us, to penetrate the veils that obscure us, and to put us in touch with the All.

"Touch" is not perhaps the right word. It is true that Being touches us and we touch it, and we speak as does Wordsworth of "a touching experience." But the word has overtones of something too transitory, of some kind of surface union only; whereas we know from our own experience that the union we seek is an ever-more penetrating oneness in which we breathe the breath of the ultimate Is-ness that flows through us as we flow through It.

The word that John Donne uses for this oneness is "interinanimating," a word in which each added prefix intensifies the sense of co-mingling: we animate one another; even more we in-animate one another; yet even

more we inter-in-animate one another — and so literally *ad infinitum.* It is this same sense of the infinite
that Yeats tries to convey when he says of the desire
for oneness that we "feel it in the deep heart's core."
Where do we feel it? In the heart. Where in the heart?
In the core of the heart. Et cetera. All of this language
is groping for a way of expressing in words that have
definite meanings an experience that is not definite but
that is literally *infinite.*

If persons are an is-ness surrounded, as it were, by
an is-not-ness, we can see why poets and philosophers
have termed the human person "an infinite in the definite" (Wordsworth and Browning), or "an infinite in
the finite" (Fichte and Hegel). We can also see why
poets, philosophers, and above all mystics can be said
to be "stammering of the ineffable" (Maréchal). How
in words that have dictionary "definitions" can one
speak of experiences that can only be called "infinitions"? Language almost breaks under this strain, as
we try to pack an infinite meaning in a finite envelope.
It is the same strain that human persons experience as
within our limited, finite nature the infinite is almost
contained.

9

Heart Speaks to Heart

THE SAME DISTINCTION THAT EXISTS between being and doing, between subject and object, between interiority and exteriority also exists between poetry and prose.

Prose is the speech of ordinary, everyday activity, the speech that is preoccupied with things and functions, with means rather than ends. As we noted in our discussion of the ineffectual infant and the omni-effective machine, the former no matter how mute and helpless is a sacred reality that must be revered as an end in itself, not as a means to something else. With persons as with poems: it does not mean, it *is* (MacLeish).

Prose as the speech of matter (which is therefore measurable) is the speech in which words have precise, objective meanings. They are *defined,* as in the dictionary. In this world of prose we mean *exactly* what we say. There are no ambiguities, no latent meanings, no revelatory overtones; prose is the speech of material exchange, of law, of commerce — ultimately of the laundry or grocery list.

But when we speak "from the heart," from the mysterious depths of what makes us to be uniquely ourselves, then our words have an inner meaning, an inner weight, an inner dimension. They are not words of the surface; they are not concerned with the veneer, the façade, the superficial, the external, the definite. The poetic word, which is simply our authentic speech, expresses our very is-ness; and just as that is-ness is infinite, so are the "meanings" of our poetic utterances.

I want to illustrate this by the word "word" itself. In the one-dimensional world of things, the world of buying and selling, of doing, making, and having, the word is reduced to a mere tag, a label, a pointer — just as in that same world people are reduced to mere means, to functionaries, to instruments.

But in the world that is the opposite of that of doing, making, and having, in the world of is-ness where we truly *are* what we are, this word "word" itself is transfigured. It is transfigured just as we are transfigured when suddenly, through the ordinary activities of the everyday humdrum, we unexpectedly experience the beauty of a person, the goodness of existence. "Transfiguration" means that our inner reality, our authentic character, shines through the veil, illuminates it so that it is no longer a veil but the medium of an epiphany of our essential is-ness. This is what the Gospel says happened to Jesus when his body was so illuminated by his inner being that what the disciples glimpsed was neither soul nor body, but only the stunning aura of both.

When we speak in these apocalyptic moments, our words are the words of full knowledge of, full love for, and full attention to (the "know, love, and serve" of that original catechetical question) the "other" whose is-ness draws us out ecstatically and into whom our own is-ness is flowing. In this unveiling moment we put off the garb, the raiment, the "fig leaves" that define our public image or persona, we put off the "uniforms" of the functionary. Rather, I should say, we do not "put off" these defining definitions, but they are transformed by the infinitions from within.

In these moments we may say, "I give you my *word.*" Here the word "word" is the same term used for all those tags and labels exchanged in the world of doing, making, and having, in the world of multiplicity. It is the same word, *but* it is utterly different. (Perhaps it may be necessary to repeat the sentence, aloud if it is helpful, to get its full significance: *I give you my word.* One could stress in five different repetitions each of the words in the sentence to get an even deeper sense of the heavy import of the whole, to get a deeper sense of the spiritual pregnancy of meaning in that final term, "I give you my *word.*")

In the heart-drawn and heart-felt moment when we say, "I give you my word," that final term, "word," is infinitely transformed. It now has a depth to it, a mysterious hidden dimension, as mysterious as the dimension of depth we experience in our own being when in the presence of beauty or goodness. If someone says in all truth, "I give you my word," we cannot define exactly, precisely what that term "word" means, because exactitude, precision reside in the world of the measurable, the material, the limited. And the term "word" in this sentence can therefore have no *definite* meaning; it has an *infinite* meaning, and therefore a meaning that transcends literal, dictionary meaning.

10

Personness Is Poemness

IT FOLLOWS FROM ALL THE ABOVE that poetry has nothing intrinsically to do with rhyme, imagery, meter, etc., anymore than the love of two persons has to do with perfume, eyeliner, or Jordache jeans. Poetry, no matter how it is couched, how it is stated, is the speech in which, as Cardinal Newman affirmed, *cor ad cor loquitur:* heart speaks to heart, the very core of our being speaks to the very core of the being of the "other." (Newman was being more pessimistic, as well as a little whimsical, when he stated that poetry is the language of childhood; prose, the language of adulthood.)

Similarly prose, no matter how it is couched, how it is stated, is the speech in which body-alone speaks to body-alone; not body transfigured by is-ness, but body envisaged as mere thing. Here there is no communication, no communion, no coming-into-oneness. Prose is the speech of two surfaces that have nothing in common except contiguity, the speech of what has been grossly but accurately called "body plumbing," the hydraulics

57

of impersonal confrontation. Prose is the speech stem-
ming from the public definitions of one another and in
which only the public (dictionary) definitions of words
are used. Poetry is the speech of the infinite, prose is the
speech of the definite. Poetry is the speech of is-ness;
prose is the speech of is-not-ness. The words may be
the same as in my examples above, but the "meanings"
are *absolutely* different.

There is no way we can force the poetic word to
be uttered, just as there is no way we can force the
experience of is-ness. As Hopkins says, "How meet
beauty? *Merely meet it.*" We cannot plan, organize,
find a method, develop a technique that will guarantee
the experience of is-ness or guarantee the speech of is-
ness. The reason for this is simple. Method, recipe,
technique exist on the plan of matter, on the plane of
the measurable and the predictable. The result of the
conjunction of two purely physical objects, say, of two
chemical elements, can be foreknown with absolute cer-
titude; the result of the conjunction of two persons can
never be predicted. When two utterly free beings come
together, two infinities meet, then the unpredictable is
raised to the nth power. Again Berdyaev: spirit is freedom.

We cannot force the experience of is-ness; we can
only let things be. Then if we *are* truly what we *are,*
again as Stevens says, "it occurs as it occurs." When we
try to force our heart to speak, when by an act of sheer
will power we try "to wear our heart on our sleeve,"
that is, when we artificially compel our being out, the
resultant speech may sound like "poetry," may sound
to those unattuned to spirit-speech as though it is gen-

uine, but it still remains the speech of the surface, of the façade. This latter is what Theodor Adorno called the "jargon of authenticity." The words, the sounds, all the *externals* of true poetry are there, all the surface elements of the speech of is-ness are there, but they are never transfigured by the real living presence of being. We have in "the jargon of authenticity" only the empty husks, the simulacrum of the genuine speech that flows "from the heart."

Cor ad cor loquitur. This cannot be faked. One may say with great ardor, in the accents of passion or excitement, "I give you my *word,*" but it will not bring about any coming into oneness, any commingling of is-ness. The empty sheath of dictionary definitions must be made pregnant with the is-ness from within. This is why the Church Fathers, following an ancient tradition, could talk of the "seeding word," the seminal word that must be planted in the ground of prosaic speech to make it truly the poetic word, the word of Being, and ultimately the Word of God.

When we speak an authentic word we speak our very selfness, and since we are attempting to exteriorize interiority, we refer to such speech as an "outering," as an "uttering." In the liturgy of the Blessed Virgin Mary the phrase attributed to her is the Psalmist's "My heart hath *uttered* a good word." The good word is not only her heartfelt assent to the message of the angel, her very is-ness responding and being drawn out (ecstasy) of her by the word of Is-ness; it is also the second person of the Trinity, who is "outered" at the birth of Jesus as her final response to the seminal word that was planted in the womb of her being at the Annunciation. It is important

to note that the translation of the Psalmist's declaration
in the Jerusalem Bible is, "A beautiful poem has welled
up from my heart." Mary's utterance is the ultimate of
authentic human speech; it represents the overflowing
of the heart and has the power to move hearts.

11

The Outering of Jesus

THREE GOSPEL EVENTS MAY BE ILLUMINATING at this
point. The first is the statement made of Jesus that he
spoke not as the scribes and pharisees, but "as one having authority." The scribes and pharisees — regardless
of what they were historically — here stand for those
whose speech does not stem from within themselves;
rather it is imitative, derivative, inauthentic, and it is
recognized as such by those who hear it. "Authority"
and "authorship" are words with the same root. True
authorship carries authority. Inauthentic speech is always a kind of plagiarism that is without power to sway
hearts. The authority of authorship means that what we
speak stems from our unique selfness.

The word that we outer is born not of things, of
surfaces, but is born of our very is-ness. As such it
is bound to be original, because each person's is-ness
is totally original — indeed, is the only original thing
about a person — totally unique; and each unique word

that we author is bound to influence others. It influences: that is, it flows into (*in-fluere*) the other person as the other person's word reciprocally flows into us. Hence, finally, the appropriateness of the liturgy's phrase of Mary, "A beautiful poem has *welled up* from my heart." The speech of is-ness is an overflowing of our very being; as such it flows into the other and has in-fluence.

Similarly, by contrast with Jesus, it was said of the scribes and pharisees that they were concerned with the minutiae of *doing.* Like Martha they lived in the world of multiplicity and business. Jesus was concerned with the *unum,* the one essential, that comes with the experience of is-ness. The essential character of the world of doing, of thingness, is brokenness, fracturedness; the essential character of the world of being, of spirit, is unity and integrity. Again, with St. Thomas, *esse et unum convertuntur:* is-ness and oneness are implicitly the same.

Third is the story of the woman healed of bleeding by Jesus. Of her it is said that she did not touch Jesus' body, nor even his hand. Even more, she did not touch his clothing; she touched only the outermost *fringe* of his clothing. The suggestion is that Jesus was so utterly filled with being that it transformed not only his physical appearance — as was visibly so at the time of the Transfiguration — but that it transformed even his clothing, even the outermost extremities of his clothing. Clothing, which from the time of the "fall" had been a sign of humanity's dual nature, now participates fully in Jesus' Is-ness. Even his veils, as it were, become transparent through the intensity of his being, so that rather than obscuring him they now become the medium of his inner power.

If clothing is the sign of humanity's duality, the sign of a discrepancy between the interior and the exterior, than here we are taught that in Jesus there is no duality whatever, no limits, no definitions. What he *appears* to be is what he really *is:* the appearance is the reality, the outside is the inside. All strain of polarities in Jesus is resolved in oneness.

Now, it is enlightening that in this gospel story Jesus himself declares that he has felt a "power" go out of him. That power, of course, is the outering of his very is-ness. And in another place it is said of him that "his speech was with power." Though there is no consistency in the use of the two Greek words in the New Testament for power, nevertheless the fact of their mere existence is significant. The one word for power is rooted in *"dyn,"* as in such words as "dynamic," "dynamite," "dynasty"; here the notion of power is basically that of physical strength or force: power that coerces and that resides primarily in the world of things. This is power that impinges only on the surface.

The second word in the New Testament for power is *"ex-ousia,"* a word with no direct English derivatives in common use, but recognizable in the Trinitarian debates of the early church that were trying to sort out whether Father and Son were of the same substance or of merely similar substance. *Ex-ousia,* then, means power flowing out of one's very substance, essence, is-ness. Jesus' speech possessed this kind of power; it influenced; it moved the heart; it did not physically coerce, it did not rely on whipping up the emotions, it did not dominate. It was the power of spiritual "inter-inanimation," the power that makes us healed, whole, and holy — all words with a common root in the idea of oneness.

12

Mortal Syntax

MOST OF OUR SPEECH is not the speech of being, substance, is-ness. It is the speech of coercion rather than of influence. It is not therefore a true "outering" because it was never really "innered." This is the speech that we think of as superficial, shallow; as concerned with surface, not with realities. "Everyday talk" is the speech that is caught up by the world of multiplicity, of the fragmented, and therefore is speech that does not transcend time, that has no trans-temporal significance. It is trapped in the quotidian, trapped in the "terrible day in and day out" of "one damned thing after another." Such talk functions on the plane of separability since it is concerned only with the material, and matter may be roughly defined as "part outside of part," fragment next to fragment, without any inner unifying principle of is-ness strongly manifest. The plane of matter, of thingness, is the plane of the "all outside," and therefore there can be no entering in. There is literally nothing to enter into because it is all surface.

All of this is brought out by our syntax. When we say, "I make a kite," or, "I kick the box," in each case we are on the plane of thingness, the plane of making and doing where subject and object are not one. There is a barrier between the "I," which is subject, and "kite" or "box," which grammatically and psychologically is called the "object." And what constitutes that barrier is *the very act* of doing, making, or having, the very act of manipulating. This is why we cannot *make* love; love is not a thing, an "it." This is why we cannot say accurately, "I possess a friend." Friends are persons, sacred realities; we do not have them, we do not possess them, nor are sacred realities things that we can "make." When we say in common speech, "Someone put the make on him," we mean someone did him evil, treated him as a thing to be manipulated, not as a person to be in-fluenced.

On the other hand, when we speak an authentic word, a true "outerance" of our "innerance" that proclaims not what we do or what we have, but what we *are,* then by its very nature as an inner reality it is *being* and it immediately brings about that unity that resides only in the domain of being. In the domain of being, "subject" and "object" are dissolved into a oneness, as when we say, "Mary *is* good." The structure is the same as "John *kicks* box," but instead of the barrier between subject and object created by the plane of doing, here on the plane of being the two are one. Mary-ness and good-ness are identical. We do not have the one over *here* and the other over *there.* In the do-

main of is-ness, the beginning and the end, the outside
and the inside, the "thou" and the "I" reside — so the
glamour of grammar tells us — in perfect mutual reci-
procity.

13

Persons and Functionaries

Even though the plane of is-ness dissolves the strain of dualities, nevertheless it is necessary to analyze such dualities. "It is necessary to distinguish," said Jacques Maritain, but ultimately only "in order to discover a higher unity."

The two fundamental categories of reality may be juxtaposed as follows, always bearing in mind the warning of Maritain that we distinguish in order to unite, and bearing in mind also that all language is inadequate to exhaust the nature of the categories to which these labels point:

interiority	exteriority
spirit	matter
unity	multiplicity
depth	surface
infinite	definite

being	doing
is-ness	is-not-ness
unpredictability	predictability
intellectus	ratio
end	means
mystery	problem
thou	it
glance	gaze

Many of these have already been introduced into this discussion, and there is an obvious hierarchy here. It is the role of the second category to be used in order to attain the first category. The first category is the category of the end-in-itself; the second category in the category of the means. The first category is the category of the sacred; the second, of the profane. What resides in the first category is Being and the transcendental expressions or aspects of being, i.e., truth, goodness, beauty, and personhood. These are all ends in themselves — hence Cardinal Newman could write a study on "knowledge as its own end." These are the realities that we seek for their own sakes, not to get anything out of them, not to do something to them, but simply because they are so infinite in worth, so rich in is-ness that they are intrinsically fascinating and alluring. The second category thus exists for the sake of the first; things exist to be used to lead us to what transcends mere thingness and use.

When someone manipulates, uses us, they are denying us our vocation to the first category. This is debasement in the deepest sense; it is evil as we defined it earlier. Even if someone says, "I love you...*because*...," there is a reduction of the sacred to the profane, there is an implicit act of debasement and manipulation. The order of "because" is always the order of functionalism. We do not love a person *because*..., since that clearly indicates that we do not love the person *as such,* but really love what the person *does* for us. If we say, "I love you because you please, comfort, console," etc., then it is the pleasure, the comfort, the consolation, etc., that we really love, and the person has been reduced to a *means* to attain those ends.

To the question of how he knew God existed and loved him, Cardinal Newman wrote in his journal, "I know because I know because I know, etc., etc., etc." The traditional sense of "proof" always entails something measurable, something quantifiable, and for that reason one cannot prove God's existence or love, since the very essence of God is to be unlimited, immeasurable. The word "measure" is related to "meter," which is related to "matter." But when we are concerned with Being/being, we are no longer on the plane of matter. There is no proving of ultimate truth, goodness, beauty; there is no proving of our relation to personhood, whether human or divine. We know because we know because... etc. Similarly, to the poet's question, "How do I love thee, let me count the ways...?" the answer can only be that they *cannot* be counted. If we say, "I love you a hundred ways," the love is limited and so rooted in matter, in the profane; if we say, a thousand ways, or even a million ways, it is still measurable, still rooted in thingness, and therefore still a debasement of the sacredness of the person who is *infinitely* lovable.

The great temptation and the great evil, as we have seen, is to treat a "thou" as "it," to treat a person as a functionary, as a surface rather than a depth, as a predictable thing rather than as a spiritual free being. But it is important to note once again that though these various categories seem to be in opposition, they really are not. Rather, they are in juxtaposition; but each category has its own proper place in the economy of existence. The category of use exists to bring us to the category of non-use, and so with all of the others.

We do not want to annihilate matter in the name of spirit, body in the name of soul. Rather, when we have attained the plane of spirit, spirit then transforms and transfigures matter, just as unity interpenetrates multiplicity. We do not want what Teilhard criticized as "unity by impoverishment," that is, unity that simply negates multiplicity or matter. We want absolute Being to transfigure contingent being without the annihilation of the latter; we want God to possess our self without the loss of that self. In fact, as we have seen earlier, when God possesses the human person, in that moment the human person becomes more fully its real self. This is the supreme paradox beyond which it is impossible for human language to go.

14

Surprise

BUT WHAT THEN CAN WE DO when we seek to utter
the word of unity, to express our very is-ness? What
must we do when we seek to truly utter our word, to
outer our in-ness? In the strict sense we can *do* nothing,
for doing, as we have noted, is always on the plane of
matter, of separability, of part outside of part. There
can be therefore no method, for method or technique is
rooted in the world of things, of multiplicity, and thus
cannot bring what the person most seeks, the plane of
unity.

When that plane is attained, we are made happy, or
rather, as Wordsworth says, we are "surprised by joy."
"Surprise" is literally *sur-prendre* (overtaken), meaning
that we are unexpectedly and unpredictably captivated
by being. We don't take it over; it both overtakes us
and takes us over. Again with Wordsworth, we don't
accurately say, "I *made* vows" — I forced by an act of
my will the sacred to manifest itself. No, rather we say,

"Vows were made for me." We can't make it happen. It happens to us.

Similarly, when Hopkins says, "a glance master more may than gaze, gaze out of countenance," he is asserting that no strained, studied effort, no methodic plodding (that is, no "gazing") can assure one of union with the "other." It is the immediate encounter, the unplanned and unplannable "glance" that alone can relate inwardness to inwardness, is-ness to is-ness. To gaze is to try to force a response from the other; it is to treat the other as a problem to be solved, rather than as a mystery to be wondered at; again, it is to reduce the other to a thing, to a functionary. We warn little children, "Don't stare at people," because staring treats the sacred person as a profane object.

We have all had the experience of trying to comprehend some truly profound idea and finding ourselves repeatedly frustrated. We keep working over the words, repeating them, analyzing their relations with one another, trying to bend them to some preconceived notion, trying to force out of them the hidden message we are sure they contain. Nothing happens. We are in the world of "gazing." We keep staring at the text. Still nothing happens. Then, perhaps out of habit, we get a cup of coffee, light a cigaret, are distracted by passersby — and suddenly, unexpectedly, the meaning comes to us. "It comes of itself." The is-ness in which this truth participates suddenly and surprisingly touches our is-ness, and in that moment, we really *know*. So, too, with a poem; so, too, with a person: they are revealed in a "glance." If we analyze, dissect, manipulate them, try to break them open to reveal something to us, nothing will happen. We rather must step back, let them speak their unique word to us; we must be attentive (they also serve who only *wait*) and silent, simply open to what is before us, and open to it on its own terms, not on ours. Then, *perhaps* (because we are still in the domain of the unpredictable) it may address us, it may reveal its inner word to us.

This is why in so many poems of union the word "unaware" is crucial. Being encounters being when we least expect it. What else could freedom, unpredictability mean? The moment of reprieve for the Ancient Mariner, the moment of death-union in "The Eve of St. Agnes," the moment of union with nature for Wordsworth's Boy of Winander—all occur in an instant of unawareness. This is another form of the *attente de Dieu.* To be unaware is not to be indifferent; on the contrary we are in a state of *attentive* expectation. We are open to what is, not in order to manipulate or force it, but simply to let it be what it is. Then its is-ness will encounter our is-ness. If we place the barrier of doing, making, "gazing," between ourselves and this "other," then we treat it as a thing, as an object to be acted upon, as a possession to own. But if we simply let ourselves *be,* and simply let the other *be,* then the joining of beings will occur. Abyss cries out to abyss: being cries out to being.

15

Letting It Be

In THIS PROCESS OF THE ENCOUNTER WITH BEING, two phrases are memorable. The first is taken from the theology of the sacraments. If the sacraments in the Christian church are conveyors of grace, then they must operate in a way parallel to the way is-ness in its "non-supernatural" dimension functions. The sacramental phrase is *nullam obicem ponere,* and it means literally "to place no obstacle." What can we *do* to receive the grace of the sacrament? We can *do* nothing. Our only role is to remove the obstacles, to let the veils down, to put aside the façade and veneer. Then, other things being equal, we can expect (*attente de Dieu*) that Being will touch our own being. We cannot guarantee it; it remains free. But we can have faith that if we are open to Being, then Being will open itself to us. Making the mute man whole and holy, Jesus said simply, "Ephphatha": *be opened.*

The very nature of being is to be diffusive; its very

nature is to seek to expand out of itself, to be one, to be one with all being. If we place no obstacle, our is-ness will be able to penetrate the masks and veils; and is-ness outside of us will be able to enter in.

The second term is *Gelassenheit,* a term put into currency by Heidegger to convey the ideal state of letting-it-be-ness, of not manipulating or coercing. When we *are* what we *are,* as we noted earlier, we intensify our is-ness. We, so to speak, "exercise" our is-ness, strengthen it so we become more truly what we are. This is candor, a condition almost of transparency whereby being flows out of us and Being flows into us.

The notion of *Gelassenheit* was not derived by Heidegger from the philosophical or from the theological tradition. It was drawn from the mystical writings of Meister Eckhart. Mysticism may be defined as the empiric psychology of union with being. *Gelassenheit* is what other mystical writers would call "holy abandonment," or the "prayer of quiet attention." In every case the emphasis is on a state of listening silence, of active "passivity," of actively letting things be what they are. Out of this silence being speaks its word to us, and we respond by speaking our word to it. And if that "it" is conceived as a something *infinitely* personal, as God, then we are in a state of mystical union.

16

Surprise Is Sursum

As we have seen, in authentic speech we experience limitlessness. Inauthentic speech affects, as it were, only the outside of us, affects only our exterior. It is not the speech of limitlessness, of the infinite; rather it is the speech that cramps and confines us and that is *lim*ited to our *limbs* — the two words are identical. It thus never reaches our "heart," the center and deepest foundation of what we are. So we tend to use expressions for authentic speech such as, "I was *deeply* moved," or "It was a *heartfelt* experience." Or with John of the Cross we say we felt it in *el profundo centro,* in the center of our being, but even more — in the deep center of our being. But if someone were to ask if that was *exactly* where we felt it, we would have to say that, no, it was even deeper than that — and even deeper than *that* that. Always there is *more,* always there is limitlessness.

This experience of the infinite "more" explains why Gabriel Marcel could call the human being a *sur-sum.*

He was thinking of the phrase in the Latin Mass, *sursum corda,* "lift up your hearts," because, as we have seen, the heart is the metaphoric foundation of our is-ness. *"Sur"* is a contraction of *"super,"* and *"sum"* means in Latin, "I am." The human person is thus defined as a "super-I am," a super being, a being that transcends its limits.

On the other hand, inauthentic speech never touches the heart because it is limited to limbs. Similarly, it is the speech that never comes from the heart, and therefore is a kind of ventriloquism, a kind of publicly spurious and derivative speech. Inauthentic speech is described rightly as "just so much static"; it never moves us, as opposed to authentic speech, which is ecstatic, welling up from our being. "Ventri-loquism" literally means "belly speech," that is, the speech of those whom we crudely but accurately describe as having "more guts than brains," more exteriority than interiority.

Finally, one can understand why the doctrine of what is called "the perpetual virginity of Mary" has been preserved by most major Christian bodies in both East and West. Doctrinal teachings maintain their vigor not merely because of the theological concepts they enforce, but also because they speak to some collective psychological need within the Christian community. It is she who is called the Blessed Virgin Mary, who "utters the good word," for virginity in its radical sense symbolizes single-mindedness and purity of intention, that is, it symbolizes oneness and integrity. Virginity signifies that state in which interiority is so diffused through exteriority that the person is "utterly" one; the word simply pours forth in the speech that we refer to as "fluent" and "influential."

Obviously I am not talking about physical virginity. One of the most venerated saints of the entire tradition in both East and West is the Magdalen — certainly not a *virgo intacta* in any gross materialistic definition — whose single-minded passion for Jesus is "virginal" in the truest sense of the word. So, too, it is the Blessed Virgin Mary who conceives in silence the greatest of ideas, and utters in silence the greatest of words.

17

Gap Leaping

WE HAVE ALREADY NOTED that poetry in its radical meaning is simply authentic speech, and prose is inauthentic speech. Thus every person outering her true is-ness is a poet, and such poetry has nothing to do with the tinsel trappings we conventionally identify with poetry.

It follows that prose, the speech of exteriority, is constrained by precise *definitions;* whereas poetry, the speech of interiority, is striving to express *infinitions,* or what Wordsworth calls "intimations of immortality." Thus teachers tell their students that in prose "you must spell everything out"; "you must be precise and exact and leave nothing to the imagination of your reader." In prose we can trace directly the process of going from A to B to C to D, etc. Prose is a linguistic chain — not unlike Blake's "mind-forged manacles" — in which every link is connected physically to every other link, part next to part, but without any transcendentally organic unity; one limb next to the other limb, one limit next to the other limit — contiguity and rubbing, but no interior relating.

In poetry, however, the teacher will tell the student, forget about exactness, definiteness: "You don't have to spell it all out. Be indirect, oblique." Again Hopkins: "where a *glance* master more may than gaze." In poetry the active intellect, the is-ness of the reader, leaps the gap from A to Z, leaps from premise to conclusion without any prosey middle term, without any physical linkage. This is why literary critics have noted that the language of poetry is "the language of ambiguity," the language that transcends dictionary *definitions* in favor of personal infinitions. Ultimately poetry seeks to dissolve all definitions of all words into the one "definition" of that Word who is by nature un-definable, who is described as the *Deus ineffabilis,* whom Rupert Brooke calls in "The Great Lover," "the inenarrable Godhead of delight."

Poetry, the speech of is-ness, is therefore intrinsically "re-ligious," because it seeks to re-ligamentize, to re-connect the multiplicity of all words so that they are fused to the one Word in which they find the ultimate ground of their true meaning. The words we all speak *as poets* are the shadow of what Stevens calls "the central Word." The words we speak *as prosaic people,* caught up in the everyday humdrum, are travesties of the central Word. Those words, as again Stevens says, are "like a body, wholly body, waving its empty sleeves." Scarecrow speech, not human speech.

18

Poems and Jokes

IN ALL THE PRECEDING DISCUSSION we have been talking of the experience of is-ness, of spirit, on a very profound level. I want now to make use of a more homely and commonplace example of the exercise of that spirit. The overall vision remains the same: what makes us happy is the authentic; what makes us unhappy is the inauthentic. What makes us happy is what makes us to be persons, "thous"; what makes us unhappy is to be excessively tinged by thingness so that we treat others and are treated by them as an object, as an "it." If spirit is utter freedom and unpredictability, and if spirit is what in the deepest dimension we *are,* then even the most ordinary experience of the unpredictable should elicit a kind of delight, not necessarily profound, not necessarily enduring, but nevertheless de-*light*-ful — an experience in which, as Wordsworth says, the "burden of the mystery in which the heavy and the weary weight of all this unintelligible world is *light*ened"; an experience in which the constraints of intractable matter are momentarily pushed aside. That experience, on the plane of the ordinary and commonplace, is the joke.

Every joke is a kind of poem, just as every poem is a kind of human person. They all exist in the world of unpredictability, and when we experience that unpredictability, we discover something to which our true nature resonates and which therefore makes us happy.

I cite a banal example: *Q.* Can a cow drink beer? *A.* Not a Holstein. When spirit "makes the connection," when spirit leaps the gap between *Holstein* and *whole stein,* then we "get" the joke. I do not want to go off on too many exemplary excursions here; Howard Nemerov has discussed in great detail such jokes.

One more equally banal illustration should be sufficient: "An African chieftain wanting to democratize his tribe decided to get rid of his throne, so he stowed it in the attic of his grass hut. Unfortunately, during a heavy storm it came crashing down to the ground floor and was smashed to pieces." *Punchline:* "People in grass houses shouldn't stow thrones." Whence the pleasure in this? Again, when we "get" it, what happens? Is it not that suddenly some uncontrollable insight leaps the gap between novel statement and hackneyed old saw? More yet: "stow thrones" is what is called a "spooner-ism," a sonic reversal, as in the reversal of "They came to scoff and stayed to pray" into "They came to cough and stayed to spray." And one can joke with the na-ture of the spoonerism — one of the lowest-level joking techniques — by defining it in high-falutin, pretentious terms as an "initial metathetic consonantal cluster."

In ordinary speech we would say that "a connection is made" when we get the joke. But what made that con-

nection can only be the free, unpredictable leap of spirit.
We have all had the experience of a joke — which I have
said is a tiny poem — that someone couldn't "get," so
we are forced to "spell it out." The process of spelling
it out, reducing it to prose, of course "kills" the joke —
just as radical thingness kills is-ness. If someone doesn't
make the leap between "People in grass houses shouldn't
stow thrones," and the old moral aphorism about people
in glass houses not throwing stones, then there is simply no way to force the insight. And if one went on to
say that in this case this does not relate to an old moral
aphorism, but to an old moral Afro-ism, and there is
still no connection made — there is nothing more one
can provide for them to "get" it. No more can one force
spirit to encounter spirit, or force another to speak an
authentic word.

Now, I want to propose a notion of God: God is
the ultimate "getter" of jokes. So intense is God's spirit
(God is defined as *Absolute* Spirit) that it is ceaselessly
leaping the gap between the most contrary and con-
tradictory things. Even the relation of Satan and the
world is for God ultimately a "joke." The flash of delight that we momentarily experience in getting the joke
is for God an enduring state; God's very nature is to
be that eternal never-ceasing incandescent luminescence
that joins infinite and finite, spirit and matter, essence
and existence — and even is-ness and notness.

When we get the joke we recognize something in
our own "psychic" makeup, something within us that
is not under the control of the conscious rational fac-
ulty and that is not subject to mere will power. We recognize something that is utterly unconstrained and un-

constrainable, utterly free. People may study the above jokes, may analyze and dissect them until they are "blue in the face" and completely embarrassed at their obtuseness. These are the people described in the complete line from Hopkins on the encounter with being: "Where a glance master more may than gaze, gaze out of countenance." "To gaze out of countenance" is to become blue in the face; it is to be embarrassed and, as we say, to lose countenance. There is no way we can force the joke — or a poem, or a person. "Never strain," wrote Baron von Hügel. Force and compulsion, as we have seen, are on the plane of matter, the plane where everything is predictable because everything is physically linked, part outside of part. This is the domain of calculative reason (ratio = measure = meter = matter). Again, one cannot prove a joke, a poem, a person. One either gets it or one doesn't. With Newman: "I know because I know because I know."

Lastly, we are delighted at this immediate recognition of a principle of utter unconstraint that transcends the limits of our everyday, harried, pressured exterior. We recognize in this uncontrollable outburst the highest reality within ourselves, a principle of free spontaneity or spirit embodied and elicited by the poem or joke.

19

Ease and Dis-ease

WE HAVE BEEN DISCUSSING freedom, spontaneity, un-predictability, *delight;* in the previous section I have stressed the last of these topics, because if our destiny is *to become what we are,* to live by our is-ness, then every experience of delight, of true joy, is an experience of that is-ness. Theodor Haecker affirmed: "Every creature that fulfills itself in joy does its own will and the will of God." To further clarify this we must look again at the glamour of grammar.

The reason I have put so much emphasis on breaking words down to their root meanings is that these meanings express something fresh and new. Words like people get trapped in habits, get reduced to the conventional and customary. Therefore we must return to the origins. It is as though whoever first created a word in some archaic setting related that word to reality in a fresh and totally original way. That primordial word was born not out of tradition, not out of what is called acculturation, but out of immediate and totally novel experience. "When in doubt etymologize," suggested Heidegger; that is, when in doubt return to the roots of thought and experience. Through such a return we may recapture something of the original naiveté with which humanity first encountered the world.

We have referred frequently to freedom, to that interior unpredictability that we recognize at the very core of our being. The term "freedom," unfortunately, is much abused and enervated. It is one of the words that Orwell used as an example of that language reduced to empty tags and labels that he called Newspeak. In Newspeak the word "freedom" had only a univocally physical meaning, as in the sentence, "The dog is free of fleas." Gone here is all sense of the mysterious burden of meanings, its archaic connotations, that the word "freedom" originally carried. For example, the suffix "dom" is related to the word "doom," not in the sense of disaster or condemnation, but in the sense of destiny, a sense that is still retained in such a word as "christen*dom*." Clearly, then, freedom in its radical meaning had a spiritual dimension that far transcended its meaning as mere "physical separation from" — as in Newspeak. The latter is simply language eviscerated, language drained of its interior value-relations.

Similarly, and more pertinent to what follows, the word "leisure" in English now conveys a state of aimless diversion, purposelessness, a condition of inertness, maybe even of sloth. But the root of leisure is *licere,* meaning "allowable." The word then is very much akin to our earlier expression, "letting-it-be-ness," although with a slightly more active connotation. Leisure in its deepest sense, then, is the state in which our ordinary

is-ness becomes more intensified, our ordinary is-ness
is "squared" or raised to the nth power — to use an earlier example. In the moment of leisure when we are
absorbed by and absorbing is-ness, then our is-ness becomes more truly what it is. Wordsworth describes persons in this state as "beings on the stretch," that is, beings reaching and being drawn out to ever more and
more fulness of is-ness. There is no other freedom, no
other *allowable* experience, than to transcend what confines us, what limits us, and to simply *be*.

The Latin word that is usually translated "leisure"
is *otium,* and this word comes into English as "ease,"
meaning that state in which everything is allowable, in
which we are truly "at ease," and where we can truly
"take it easy." The opposite of this state of *otium* is
neg-otium: the condition of unrest in which we carry
on the *business* of doing, making, and having, and in
which we are limited to our limbs, and enslaved by the
world of matter. Nothing is more enslaved than that
which cannot escape from its own confines, from what
Milton calls the "dark-some house of mortal clay."

Unfortunately, that phrase of Milton's is probably
too negative, too redolent of a puritanic fear of the body.
For it is not a question of putting aside the body, but
rather of "transubstantiating" it. A better description of
the body is Hopkins's sacramental notion of it as "the
mean house" — a phrase that seems to echo Milton's.
But in fact Hopkins does not use "mean" to express con-
tempt or disdain; he is much too holistic a Christian for
that. "Mean" here is used as in mathematics to express
the medium, the intermediate. The body is seen as the
intermediate reality that in this present phase of exis-

tence encompasses is-ness, but that in "the next phase" will be not antagonistic or juxtaposed, but simply the external manifestation of that is-ness. Though the body in this life is often refractory (e.g., St. Francis's "Brother Ass") in the next life the "risen body," says Hopkins, will be to our is-ness as a rainbow is to the field it rests on: something that beautifies and enhances.

Otium is the state in which the tension between spirit and matter, soul and body, no longer exists. The whole person is "at ease." Here we can recognize the import of Augustine's celebrated injunction, "Love, and do what you want"; because in these moments of leisure everything is licit.

Obviously there are some qualifications called for here. There is in the Catholic tradition, and it is reduplicated in various forms both within Protestantism and Orthodoxy, a heresy called Quietism. Like most heresies and "phantom heresies" it was the exaggeration of a legitimate tendency and was probably rarely followed to its logical extremes. But what it did suggest, among other things, was that in certain states of contemplation, the soul enjoyed so intimate a union with God that the body might lapse into objectively sinful acts without the person incurring any guilt.

Though the heresy was condemned for rendering the sacraments needless and for fostering potential licentiousness, the real evil was its extreme dualism, a dualism that is the contradiction of everything indicated above.

Thus it would be a serious error to read Augustine's statement in any Quietistic fashion. Rather, what Augustine and the central tradition maintained is that in

the moments of highest union the soul and the body are
so integrated that all dualism is resolved. Similarly in
those moments *what ever we do* will be an act of love.
(Sadly, one of the last acts of anti-Quietist Inquisitors
was the silencing of the great Mexican poet, Sor Juana
Inés de la Cruz.) What the Quietists were experiencing
was not the true *otium sanctum* of the Church Fathers,
the true ease in which body and soul are utterly integrated. Rather, they were experiencing that separation
between soul and body which, as we have noted above,
is really *neg-otium,* a word that is usually translated as
"business," but that can be more accurately and literally
translated as *dis-ease,* the absence of real holiness and
wholeness and health.

In the poetic tradition, and in much of the religious
tradition as well, the ultimate act of leisure is when we
definitively put off all that confines us, that is, when we
put off our limbs that limit us. This is death, which like
all mysteries is at once awesome and fascinating, terrifying and attractive. Nor do we have to envision death
according to the somewhat Platonic model of Karl Rah-
ner to realize that it entails the transcending of limits.
We know this from experience. And that is one reason why authentic sexual communion — when we truly
outer our word through our bodies so that we are one
with the is-ness of the other — has for hundreds of years
in the poetry of the West been compared to the act of
dying.

Thus Keats, while describing at once actually dying
and being sexually united, declares of the hero of the
"The Eve of St. Agnes," "... into her dream he melted
as the rose blendeth its odor with the violet." He then

adds: "solution sweet" — in this moment all problems are resolved, all questions are answered, all oppositions are ended, all dualities are fused. It is a sweet solution to them all, a sweet resolution, and a sweet flowing of being into being, and of being into Being. For these same reasons in the Nightingale Ode, Keats speaks of loving "easeful death," loving that death which is the ultimate act of ease, of *otium,* and which puts the quietus to the dis-ease, the *negotium* and busy-ness of this world.

20

Ease-ness as Is-ness

I HAVE CITED HOPKINS FREQUENTLY as the poet of
what might be called the "first naiveté," the poet who
seems to have looked upon the world with the innocence
of a newborn child or the simplicity of an untouched
archaic intelligence. Hopkins, like an Adam dreaming,
awoke and found it truth. If Hopkins has a counterpart
in this candor, it is another priest poet, George Herbert,
who has a characteristically touching ("touching" because it enters into us) and moving ("moving" because
it ecstatically attracts us) poem called after the Holy
Name: "Iesu." In it he tells how the Holy Name was
inscribed in his heart, but after he had sinned the name
was broken up into tiny pieces and scattered about.
Then after he had repented and been forgiven, he went
to pick up the pieces of the Holy Name (and of his life)
in order to put the Holy Name (and himself) together
again. When he had reassembled the pieces of the name,
he saw that it spelled correctly "IESU"; but then he saw
the old breaks still showing between the letters, and he

realized that what it also spelt was I ES U. This he immediately recognized as the voice of Jesus saying, "I
ease you." What does the Is-ness of God do to our is-
ness? It gives us the freedom of the children of God,
the true *ease* that dispels the shadows of the world of
neg-otium and dis-ease.

Herbert's poem is one extended pun on the Holy
Name; the surface level of that pun is examined above.
But there is an even deeper level, and as should not be
surprising this deeper level is that of is-ness. Here the
sentence "I ease you" is also the sentence "I is you,"
meaning first, in the words of Augustine, "God became
man in order that man might become God," and second, that the Is-ness of God is somehow the is-ness of
the human person.

Hence the significance of the seeming grammatical
error. Its function is to emphatically underscore that
it is is-ness that God and the human person have "in
common," that they are *related* by what is called the
"analogy of is-ness." For a similar reason, but abstract-
ing from the supernatural, the French poet Arthur Rimbaud makes the same grammatical error when he writes,
"Je *est* un autre," literally, "I *is* another." Neither "am"
in English nor "suis" in French suggests the connection with is-ness that these two grammatically "wrong"
verbs do. Another way of saying "I is you" is that of
the Catechism of the Council of Trent: "While retain-
ing their own substance, those who delight in God do
assume a certain and properly divine form, and they
may be regarded as Gods rather than as human beings."

And so, we can now say more completely and more

accurately in reply to our initial question, "Why did God make us?" that the answer is: God made us that we might become God while becoming more fully our real selves.

Suggested Readings

THIS IS NOT A BIBLIOGRAPHY in the standard sense; it is precisely what the title indicates, additional books that in their own particular ways focus on the central themes discussed above. Each book is relatively short, and each is philosophically and religiously helpful. I am providing only author and title because some of these books have gone through different editions, and some are out of print, but available at most college libraries.

The Bourgeois Mind, by Nicholas Berdyaev. Although written more than fifty years ago, this critique of modern society is more relevant than ever. The author comes out of a rich tradition combining Russian Orthodoxy, classical Gnosticism, Platonism, and anti-Sovietism.

I and Thou, by Martin Buber. Anchored in the Hebrew Bible, this is a classic religious and philosophic work on interpersonal relations, both individual and collective. Its language and its insights have been utilized throughout the pages above.

Man's Search for Meaning, by Victor Frankl. A work of depth-psychology affirming the goal of existence tested by the author's own experiences in Hitler's death camps and in his practice as a therapist.

The Christian Imagination, by Justus George Lawler. Two of the studies in this book are incorporated in much of the discussion above: "The Christian Formation of Youth"; "The Christian Understanding of Love."

Homo Viator, by Gabriel Marcel. The title means "wayfarer"; the book elaborates the distinction between problem and mystery in the context of Christian existentialism.

One-Dimensional Man, by Herbert Marcuse. A humanist-Marxist analysis of contemporary culture, particularly American culture; the treatment of the degradation of language and its impoverishment is remarkably acute.

Presence of the Word, by Walter J. Ong, S.J. "Word" here is the word of human speech, the poetic word, and the Word of the Christian Trinity. The book is rich in historical illustrations of the revolution accompanying the development of printing technology.

Leisure the Basis of Culture, by Joseph Pieper. A book of two essays; the title essay illuminates the "contemplative" goal of human existence; of the second and more important essay, "The Philosophical Act," it is not too much to say that if one understands it thoroughly, one will have grasped the foundations of Western philosophy.

The Divine Milieu, by Pierre Teilhard de Chardin, S.J. In an incandescent style a priest-scientist here shows that one's human work is intrinsically noble and that by enriching the world, one "enriches" God.

Liturgy and Personality, by Dietrich von Hildebrand. In the context of Catholic worship, this book shows that it is those things to which we devote ourselves *for their own sakes* that have the deepest formative effect on our personal development.